MONETIZE
LIKE A BOSS

YOUTUBE'S 30-DAY MONEYMAKING ROADMAP

Table of Contents

Introduction

Welcome to the thrilling world of YouTube, where dreams can become reality, and passions can turn into profits. If you've ever envisioned transforming your love for creating videos into a lucrative endeavor, you're about to embark on a remarkable journey. The goal? To monetize your YouTube channel in just 30 days. Yes, you read that correctly - a mere 30 days to start generating income from your content.

As you dive into this adventure, keep in mind that it's not an elusive aspiration but an attainable objective. The digital landscape has evolved, providing new and exciting opportunities for content creators. With the right strategies and dedication, you can unlock the potential of your YouTube channel and begin reaping the rewards sooner than you might think.

YouTube has emerged as a powerful platform for individuals to express their creativity, share their knowledge, and connect with a global audience. It's not just a platform for viewing cat videos or funny skits; it's a vast ecosystem with niches covering virtually every topic imaginable. Whether you're passionate about technology, cooking, travel, beauty, or any other subject, there's an audience out there eager to engage with your content.

This guide will serve as your roadmap to success. It will take you through the intricacies of YouTube monetization, starting with the fundamental concepts and eligibility criteria. You'll discover the importance of creating high-quality, engaging content that resonates with your target audience. Effective channel optimization, branding, and video promotion strategies will be unveiled, providing you with the tools to stand out in the crowded YouTube landscape.

Monetization, the ultimate goal, will be explored in detail. From setting up Google AdSense for ad revenue to exploring affiliate marketing, you'll learn how to maximize your income potential.

But success on YouTube isn't solely about revenue; it's also about adhering to YouTube's policies and community guidelines, ensuring a safe and respectful environment for your audience.

The heart of this guide lies in the 30-day action plan, a step-by-step journey that will take you from a budding content creator to a monetization-ready YouTube channel owner. We'll break down the process into manageable phases, from content creation to audience building, and guide you through each day's tasks.

As you progress through this journey, remember that YouTube is a dynamic platform. The key to success is adaptability and continuous improvement. We'll discuss how to measure your success through analytics and insights, enabling you to fine-tune your strategy as you gain more experience.

By the end of this 30-day adventure, you'll be equipped with the knowledge and skills needed to monetize your YouTube channel. You'll have the confidence to create, optimize, and promote your content effectively, all while complying with YouTube's guidelines.

So, are you ready to take the plunge and unlock the potential of your YouTube channel? Fasten your seatbelt, grab your camera, and let's embark on this exciting journey to monetize your YouTube channel in just 30 days.

We understand that getting monetized is not an easy task. But there's good news! At the end of the book we have provided an email address. Kid you'd like for us to boost your channel's views and subscriptions that'll qualify you for monetization in 2 to 4 weeks, simply send us an email. Now let the money-making begin.

Chapter 1

Understanding YouTube Monetization

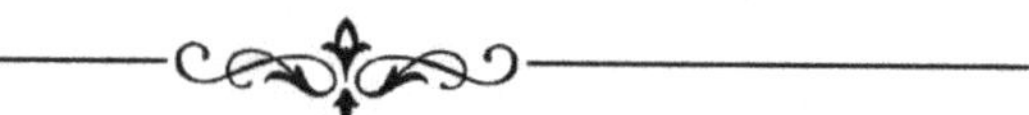

Before we dive into the nitty-gritty of YouTube monetization, it's crucial to grasp the fundamental concepts and the potential it holds. You may have already seen success stories of YouTubers making a living from their channels, but how does it all work, and is it really achievable for everyone?

YouTube monetization is the process of earning money from your videos and channel. The primary way this is done is through the YouTube Partner Program (YPP), which allows you to monetize your videos with ads and access other revenue-generating features on the platform. But before you can join the YPP, you need to meet certain eligibility requirements set by YouTube.

Understanding the Eligibility Criteria:

To be eligible for the YPP, you need to fulfill these basic requirements:

Watch Hours: Your channel must have accumulated at least 4,000 watch hours in the last 12 months.

Subscribers: You should have a minimum of 1,000 subscribers.

Adherence to YouTube Policies: Your content must comply with YouTube's Community Guidelines, AdSense Program Policies, and other content policies.

Copyright and Community Strikes: You shouldn't have any severe or repeated copyright strikes or community guideline strikes on your channel.

It's essential to understand that these requirements are in place to ensure that creators who monetize are offering valuable and compliant content to their audience. Meeting these thresholds signifies that you have gained a certain level of trust with YouTube and its viewers.

Why Is Monetization Valuable?

Now, you might wonder why you should be so keen on monetizing your YouTube channel. The answer is simple: monetization enables you to turn your passion into a profession. It allows you to dedicate more time and resources to creating content that resonates with your audience, all while earning a steady income.

Monetization also provides the opportunity to reinvest in your channel, improving the quality of your videos, and reaching a broader audience. It's a rewarding cycle where success breeds more success. However, it's not just about the money; it's about pursuing what you love and making a positive impact on others through your content.

The Journey to Monetization:

Understanding YouTube monetization is the first step on your journey. In the following chapters, we will delve into the specifics of how to meet the eligibility criteria, optimize your content, and strategically grow your channel to fulfill your dreams of becoming a monetized YouTuber. This book will be your comprehensive guide, providing you with the tools and knowledge to make this dream a reality. So, let's embark on this exciting journey together!

Chapter 2

Setting Up Your YouTube Channel for Success

In the previous chapter, we introduced you to the world of YouTube and the exciting potential it offers for content creators. Now, it's time to take action and set up your YouTube channel for success. Whether you're starting from scratch or looking to

optimize an existing channel, this chapter will guide you through the essential steps to establish a strong foundation for your YouTube journey.

The Importance of a Well-Structured Channel

Your YouTube channel serves as your digital identity on the platform. It's where you showcase your content, engage with your audience, and build your brand. A well-structured channel not only attracts viewers but also convinces them to subscribe and keep coming back for more. Here's why it's crucial:

> First Impressions: Your channel's appearance and organization make the first impression on potential viewers. A professional and inviting channel layout sets the tone for your content.

Trust and Credibility: A well-structured channel conveys trust and credibility. It shows that you're serious about your content and committed to your audience. Audience Retention: Viewers are more likely to explore your content when they find your channel visually appealing and easy to navigate. This can lead to longer watch times and more engagement.

Monetization Opportunities: If your goal is to monetize your channel, a well-structured channel is a prerequisite. Meeting YouTube's Partner Program requirements, which we'll discuss later, is much easier with a professional channel setup.

Steps to Set Up Your YouTube Channel for Success

Now, let's dive into the steps to set up your YouTube channel for success:

1. Create a Google Account

Before you can create a YouTube channel, you'll need a Google account. If you already have a Google account, you can use it to log in to YouTube. If not, you can easily create one. Your Google account will serve as the foundation for managing your channel.

2. Choose Your Channel Name

Your channel name is your brand's identity on YouTube. It should be unique, memorable, and relevant to your content. Consider a name that reflects your niche or the type of content you'll produce. Ensure that it's easy to spell and not too long.

3. Customize Your Channel

Customization is where you make your channel visually appealing. Here's what you should do:

- Profile Picture: Upload a profile picture. This could be your face, a logo, or an image representing your brand. Make sure it's clear and recognizable, even insmaller sizes.
- Channel Banner: Create a channel banner that visually represents your content. You can include your channel name and a brief description. The banner should bethe right size for all devices.
- Channel Description: Write a compelling channel description. In a few sentences, explain what your channel is about and what viewers can expect. This is your
  elevator pitch to potential subscribers.

4. Set Up Your Channel Trailer

Your channel trailer is like a movie trailer for your content. It's a short video that introduces new visitors to your channel. Use this opportunity to tell them what your channel is about, why they should subscribe, and what they can expect from your videos. A well-made channel trailer can significantly impact whether a viewer decides to subscribe or not.

5. Understand Your Niche

Understanding your niche is essential. A niche is the specific focus or subject matter of your channel. It's what sets you apart from other creators. Take the time to research and define your niche. What are you passionate about, and what do you want to share with the world? The clearer your niche, the easier it is to attract a dedicated audience.

6. Plan Your Content

A content strategy is your roadmap for what you'll create. It includes the type of videos you'll make, the topics you'll cover, and the schedule for publishing. Planning your content in advance ensures that you always have ideas and never miss posting.

7. Understand YouTube Policies

YouTube has specific policies and guidelines that all creators must follow. It's essential to be aware of these policies, which include Community Guidelines, AdSense Program Policies, and copyright rules. Violating these policies can lead to channel strikes and even removal, so make sure you understand and adhere to them.

8. Familiarize Yourself with YouTube Studio

YouTube Studio is your command center for channel management. It allows you to upload and manage videos, view analytics, and interact with your audience. Take some time to explore YouTube Studio and get comfortable with its features.

9. Verify Your Channel

Verifying your channel adds an extra layer of authenticity. It's a straightforward process that involves receiving a verification code from Google and entering it on your YouTube channel. A verified channel is more trusted by viewers and is a step toward unlocking certain features.

10. Branding and Thumbnails

Consistency in branding is key. Create a visual identity for your channel, including color schemes and graphics that match your content. Design eye-catching thumbnails for your videos. Thumbnails are the first things viewers see, and they play a significant role in click-through rates.

11. Optimize for SEO

Understanding Search Engine Optimization (SEO) for YouTube is essential. Use relevant keywords in your video description, tags, and closed captions to improve discoverability. SEO plays a crucial role in reaching a broader audience.

12. Set Your Channel Defaults

YouTube allows you to set defaults for video uploads. This includes default video titles, descriptions, and tags. It's a time-saving feature that ensures consistency in your video metadata.

13. Customize Your URL

Once your channel is eligible, you can customize your channel's URL. This makes it easier for viewers to find you. Choose a custom URL that aligns with your channel name and is easy to remember.

14. Connect with Social Media

Promote your channel through your social media accounts. Cross-promotion can help you reach a broader audience and bring in viewers who are already interested in your niche.

15. Upload Your First Video

Now, it's time to upload your first video. Use the knowledge you've gained so far to create a compelling video. Pay attention to the details: video quality, audio quality, editing, and engaging content.

By following these steps, you'll set up a YouTube channel that not only looks professional but is also poised for growth. The next chapters will delve into the specifics of creating high-quality content, building your audience, and monetizing your channel.

Stay committed, and success on YouTube is well within reach

Chapter 3

Creating High-Quality Content for Your YouTube Channel

In Chapter 2, we discussed the essential steps to set up your YouTube channel for success. Now that you have a well-structured channel, it's time to focus on the heart of your content creation journey—creating high-quality videos. The success of your YouTube channel depends largely on the content you produce. This chapter will guide you through the process of crafting engaging, informative, and visually appealing videos that captivate your audience.

Understanding the Importance of High-Quality Content

Creating high-quality content is not just a suggestion; it's a necessity. YouTube is a platform where millions of videos compete for viewers' attention. To stand out, your content must be exceptional. Here's why it's crucial:

Steps to Create High-Quality YouTube Content

Now, let's dive into the steps to create high-quality YouTube content:

1. Define Your Niche and Audience

Before you start producing content, you must know your niche and target audience. Your niche defines the type of content you'll create, and your target audience determines who your videos are intended for. Research your niche thoroughly, understand your competitors, and identify your audience's preferences.

2. Plan Your Content

A content strategy is crucial for consistent and effective content creation. Plan your videos in advance, outlining the topics, format, and publishing schedule. A

well-thought-out content calendar ensures that you always have ideas and never miss posting.

3. Script and Storyboard

For more structured content, such as tutorials or storytelling, scripting and storyboarding are essential. A script ensures your narrative is clear and concise, while a storyboard helps visualize the video's flow and shots.

4. Invest in Quality Equipment

While you don't need the most expensive gear, investing in decent recording equipment and software is necessary. A good camera, microphone, and video editing software can significantly improve your video quality.

5. Lighting and Sound

Proper lighting and audio quality are often underestimated. Well-lit scenes and clear sound enhance the viewing experience. Invest in good lighting equipment and ensure you record in a quiet environment.

6. Editing and Post-Production

Video editing is where you can polish your content. Trim unnecessary parts, add

transitions, graphics, and music to make your video more engaging. Learning how to edit is a valuable skill for any YouTuber.

7. Thumbnails and Titles

Your video's thumbnail and title are what potential viewers see first. They must be eye-catching and represent the video's content accurately. Learn to create appealing thumbnails and use keyword-rich titles.

8. Engaging Introductions

Grab your viewers' attention right from the start. An engaging introduction sets the tone for the video and encourages viewers to stay.

9. Content Value

Deliver value in your content. Whether it's entertainment, education, or inspiration, ensure that viewers gain something from watching your videos. Be authentic and passionate about your subject.

10. Calls to Action (CTAs)

Encourage viewer engagement by using effective CTAs. Ask viewers to like, subscribe, comment, and share your videos. Interaction with your audience is key to building a community.

11. Optimize for SEO

Understanding Search Engine Optimization (SEO) for YouTube is essential. Use relevant keywords in your video description, tags, and closed captions to improve discoverability.

12. Consistency

Consistency is vital in building your audience. Stick to your content calendar and engage with your viewers regularly.

13. Monitor Analytics

YouTube provides valuable analytics data. Pay attention to watch time, audience retention, and viewer demographics. This information can guide your content strategy.

Creating high-quality content takes time and effort, but it's a rewarding endeavor.

Remember that practice makes perfect, and you'll improve with each video you create. Stay committed to your channel's growth, and you'll see results over time.

Conclusion

In this chapter, we've emphasized the importance of creating high-quality content for your YouTube channel. From defining your niche to understanding the nuances of video production, these steps are the foundation of your content creation journey. With dedication and a commitment to improving your skills, you can produce videos that not only attract viewers but also keep them coming back for more.

In the next chapter, we'll explore the critical aspect of building your brand and audience on YouTube, which complements your content creation efforts. Stay tuned for more insights and strategies to help you achieve success on your YouTube journey.

Chapter 4

Optimizing Your YouTube Videos for Maximum Visibility

You've set up your YouTube channel, and you're ready to share your content with the world. But in the vast sea of online videos, how do you ensure that your content reaches your target audience? The answer lies in optimizing your YouTube videos for maximum visibility. In this chapter, we'll explore the strategies and techniques that can help your videos stand out and get the attention they deserve.

The Power of YouTube SEO

YouTube is the second-largest search engine in the world, right after Google. People come to YouTube not only for entertainment but also to find answers, learn new skills, and explore various topics. To make your videos discoverable, you need to harness the power of YouTube SEO (Search Engine Optimization).

What is YouTube SEO?

YouTube SEO involves using various strategies to make your videos more search-friendly and appealing to both viewers and YouTube's algorithms. By optimizing your videos, you increase the likelihood of them appearing in search results, recommendations, and suggested videos.

Keyword Research

Keyword research is at the heart of YouTube SEO. Start by identifying relevant keywords that describe your video content. You can use tools like Google's Keyword Planner, YouTube's auto-suggest feature, or dedicated keyword research tools. Look for keywords with a good search volume but not too much competition.

Optimizing Video Titles

Your video title is one of the first things viewers see. It should be clear, concise, and include your target keyword. A compelling title not only grabs attention but also helps with SEO. Avoid clickbait titles that mislead viewers, as this can hurt your channel's reputation.

Writing Informative Descriptions

The video description is your opportunity to provide more context about your video.

Include relevant keywords and a brief summary of the video's content. You can also include links to your website or social media profiles. A well-written description not only helps with SEO but also enhances the viewer's experience.

Video Tags

Tags are another essential element for YouTube SEO. These are additional keywords that further describe your video's content. Use a mix of broad and specific tags, including variations and synonyms of your target keyword. Tags help YouTube understand the context of your video.

Eye-Catching Thumbnails

Thumbnails play a significant role in click-through rates. Create custom thumbnails that are visually appealing and relevant to your video. Use contrasting colors and include text or graphics to highlight the video's topic. An attractive thumbnail encourages viewers to click.

Closed Captions

Adding closed captions to your videos not only makes them more accessible but also improves SEO. YouTube's algorithms can crawl and index captions, making your video content more searchable. Additionally, captions benefit viewers who prefer to watch videos with the sound off.

User Engagement

User engagement is a critical factor in YouTube's ranking algorithm. Videos that receive likes, comments, shares, and longer watch times are considered more valuable by YouTube. Here's how you can encourage user engagement:

Call to Action (CTA)

Use calls to action in your videos to prompt viewers to like, subscribe, comment, and share. Engage with your audience by responding to comments and building a community around your channel.

Watch Time

Encourage longer watch times by creating engaging content that retains viewer interest. Avoid lengthy introductions and get to the point quickly. Keep your content informative and entertaining throughout.

Share on Social Media

Promote your videos on your social media platforms. Sharing your content on Facebook, Twitter, Instagram, and other social networks can bring in more viewers and increase engagement.

Analytics and Iteration

YouTube provides valuable analytics data that can help you refine your video content and SEO strategy. Pay attention to metrics such as watch time, audience retention, and click-through rates. Use this data to make informed decisions about your content and improve over time.

Consistency

Consistency is key on YouTube. Stick to a regular posting schedule so that viewers know when to expect new content. Building a loyal audience depends on your ability to deliver content consistently.

Mobile Optimization

Many viewers access YouTube on mobile devices. Ensure that your videos are

mobile-friendly. Use readable fonts, and design thumbnails and graphics that look good on smaller screens.

Conclusion

Optimizing your YouTube videos for maximum visibility is an ongoing process. By incorporating the strategies mentioned in this chapter, you can increase the chances of your content being discovered by a wider audience. Remember that YouTube SEO, user engagement, and consistent posting are the pillars of a successful YouTube channel.

In the next chapter, we'll explore the art of building and engaging with your YouTube audience. Creating a community around your channel is not only fulfilling but also crucial for long-term success. Stay tuned for more insights and strategies on your YouTube journey.

Chapter 5

Engaging Your YouTube Audience and Building a Community

Congratulations on optimizing your YouTube videos for maximum visibility in the

previous chapter. Now, it's time to focus on one of the most crucial aspects of your YouTube journey—engaging your audience and building a community around your channel. A loyal and engaged audience can make the difference between a successful YouTube channel and one that struggles to gain traction.

The Importance of Audience Engagement

Audience engagement goes beyond just accumulating views and likes. It's about creating a two-way interaction with your viewers. Engaged audiences are more likely to:

- Subscribe: Viewers who feel a connection with your content are more likely to hit that subscribe button, ensuring they don't miss any of your future videos.

- Comment: Comments provide an opportunity for viewers to express their thoughts, ask questions, and share their experiences related to your content.

• Share: Engaged viewers are more inclined to share your videos on social media or with friends, expanding your reach.

• Participate: Engagement can involve participation in polls, challenges, and contests you host on your channel.

Building a Community

Creating a community around your YouTube channel is about fostering a sense of belonging and shared interests among your viewers. When your audience feels like they are part of a community, they are more likely to stay engaged and continue supporting your channel. Here's how to build a community:

Interact with Comments

Always respond to comments on your videos. This shows that you value your viewers' opinions and encourages more interaction. Ask questions in your video descriptions or verbally in your videos to prompt comments.

Host Live Streams

Live streaming is a powerful tool for real-time interaction with your audience. Use live streams for Q&A sessions, behind-the-scenes looks, or just casual chats. Announce live streams in advance to give your viewers time to join.

Create a Posting Schedule

Consistency is key to building a community. Establish a regular posting schedule so viewers know when to expect new content. This keeps them coming back for more and creates a sense of anticipation.

Collaborate with Viewers

Involve your viewers in your content creation process. You can ask for video ideas, conduct polls to decide on topics, or even feature user-generated content in your videos.

Social Media Presence

Maintain an active presence on social media platforms. Share updates, engage with your audience, and promote your videos. Cross-promotion between YouTube and social media can help grow your community.

Exclusive Content

Consider offering exclusive content or perks to your most dedicated viewers. This could include early access to videos, behind-the-scenes content, or special badges for channel members.

Handling Criticism

Not all engagement will be positive, and it's important to know how to handle criticism and negative comments. Here are some tips:

- Stay Professional: Maintain a professional tone in your responses and avoid getting defensive.

- Filter Constructive Feedback: Differentiate between constructive criticism and hate comments. Constructive feedback can help you improve.

- Moderate Your Comments: Use YouTube's comment moderation tools to filter out inappropriate or offensive comments.

- Don't Engage in Arguments: Avoid getting into arguments with negative commenters. It rarely leads to a positive outcome.

Analytics and Feedback

Regularly review your YouTube analytics to gain insights into what's working and what's not. Pay attention to metrics like watch time, audience retention, and click-through rates. You can use this data to adjust your content and engagement strategies.

Conclusion

Building an engaged audience and community around your YouTube channel is a rewarding and ongoing process. By interacting with your viewers, creating a sense of belonging, and offering consistent, high-quality content, you can foster a dedicated following. Remember, the key to success on YouTube is not just about the numbers; it's about the meaningful connections you create with your audience.

In the next chapter, we'll explore strategies for monetizing your YouTube channel. It's an exciting step for those who want to turn their passion for creating content into a source of income. Stay tuned for more insights and tips on your YouTube journey.

Chapter 6

Monetizing Your YouTube Channel

Up to this point in your YouTube journey, you've learned how to optimize your channel, create engaging content, and build a loyal audience. Now, it's time to explore the exciting world of monetization. This chapter will guide you through the various ways you can turn your YouTube channel into a source of income.

Why Monetize Your Channel?

Monetizing your YouTube channel can offer several benefits:

Earn Money: The most obvious reason is to generate income from your content. You can turn your passion into a profitable venture.

Full-Time Career: Successful YouTubers often transition into full-time content creation, allowing them to focus entirely on their channel.

Invest in Quality: Monetization provides funds to improve the quality of your content, invest in better equipment, and hire assistance if needed.

Diversify Income: YouTube can become one of several income streams, reducing financial dependency on a single source.

YouTube Partner Program (YPP)

To start earning money on YouTube, you'll need to join the YouTube Partner Program. Here are the eligibility requirements:

- Have at least 1,000 subscribers.

- Have at least 4,000 watch hours in the past 12 months.

- Comply with all YouTube policies and guidelines.

Once you meet these criteria, you can apply for the YPP. Once accepted, you can start earning money through:

1.   Ad Revenue

You can enable ads on your videos, and you'll earn a share of the revenue generated by these ads. The more views and engagement your videos get, the more ad revenue you can earn.

2.   Channel Memberships

You can offer channel memberships to your subscribers for a monthly fee. Subscribers get access to exclusive badges, emojis, and members-only content.

### 3.	Super Chat and Super Stickers

These features allow your live stream viewers to pay to highlight their messages or send animated stickers. It's a great way to earn during live streams.

Sponsored Content

Collaborating with brands can be a lucrative way to make money on YouTube. Here's how it works:

> Brand Partnerships: Companies pay you to create content that promotes their products or services. It can include dedicated videos, product placements, or mentions.

> Affiliate Marketing: You promote a product or service and earn a commission for every sale made through your unique affiliate link.

> Sponsored Videos: Brands pay you to create videos centered around their products or themes.

When working with sponsors, it's essential to maintain transparency with your audience and only promote products or services that align with your channel's niche and your viewers' interests.

Merchandise Sales

Many YouTubers design and sell merchandise related to their channel. This can include T-shirts, hats, mugs, or any other custom items. Platforms like Teespring and Printful make it easy to create and sell your merchandise.

Crowdfunding

Crowdfunding platforms like Patreon and Ko-fi allow your most dedicated viewers to support your channel by making regular donations. In return, you can offer exclusive content, early access, or personalized shout-outs.

Premium Content

You can offer premium content that viewers can access for a fee. This can include online courses, ebooks, or in-depth tutorials related to your channel's niche.

Public Speaking and Workshops

As your channel grows, you may be invited to speak at events or host workshops related to your expertise. Public speaking engagements and workshops can be a significant source of income.

Book Deals and Licensing

If your YouTube channel revolves around a specific topic, you might have the opportunity to write a book or license your content to other platforms or media outlets.

Building Multiple Income Streams

Successful YouTubers often combine several income streams to create a stable financial foundation. Building a diversified income portfolio can help you weather fluctuations in ad revenue and audience engagement.

Legal and Financial Considerations

Monetizing your YouTube channel also comes with legal and financial responsibilities. You should:

- . Keep track of your earnings and expenses. Understand tax implications.
- . Familiarize yourself with copyright laws and fair use policies.
- . Consider forming a legal business entity if your channel grows significantly.

Conclusion

Monetizing your YouTube channel is an exciting step in your content creator journey.

However, it's crucial to maintain the same passion and authenticity that drew viewers to your channel in the first place. Your audience should always be at the center of your content and monetization strategies. As you explore various income streams, remember that building a sustainable, long-term career on YouTube requires dedication, creativity, and a deep connection with your audience.

In the next chapter, we'll delve into the evolving world of YouTube trends and strategies. Stay tuned for more insights and tips to keep your channel thriving in the ever-changing digital landscape.

Chapter 7

Effective Time Management

In today's fast-paced world, effective time management is a critical skill. Whether you're a student, a professional, an entrepreneur, or someone looking to make the most out of their day, mastering time management can significantly impact your productivity and quality of life. This chapter explores the principles, techniques, and tools you need to manage your time efficiently.

Understanding Time Management

Time management is the process of planning and organizing your tasks and activities to maximize productivity and achieve your goals. It involves prioritizing, setting goals, and making the best use of your available time. Effective time management allows you to:

> Increase Productivity: You can accomplish more in less time.

> Reduce Stress: Knowing you have control over your schedule can lower stress levels.

> Achieve Goals: You can work towards your personal and professional objectives. Improve Work-Life Balance: Balancing work, family, and personal time becomes more manageable.

The Principles of Effective Time Management

To become proficient at time management, you need to understand and apply several key principles:

1. Set Clear Goals

Clear, well-defined goals give your tasks purpose. Knowing what you want to achieve helps you prioritize your time effectively. Consider both short-term and long-term goals.

2. Prioritize Tasks

Not all tasks are equally important. Use methods like the Eisenhower Matrix

(categorizing tasks into urgent/important, not urgent/important, urgent/not important, and not urgent/not important) to identify priorities.

3. Plan Your Day

Start your day with a plan. Create a to-do list or schedule your tasks in a planner. Allocating specific time slots for each task ensures that you don't waste time.

4. Avoid Multitasking

Multitasking can reduce efficiency. Focus on one task at a time, complete it, and then move on to the next. This method is known as "single-tasking."

5. Use Time Management Tools

Various tools and techniques can help you manage your time efficiently. These include digital calendars, task management apps, and the Pomodoro Technique (working for 25 minutes, then taking a 5-minute break).

6. Learn to Say No

Sometimes, you have to decline additional tasks or commitments to protect your time. Learning to say no is a vital skill in time management.

7. Avoid Procrastination

Procrastination is a time thief. Combat it by breaking tasks into smaller, more manageable parts and tackling them one step at a time.

8. Delegate

Don't hesitate to delegate tasks when possible. Delegating can free up your time to focus on more critical responsibilities.

9. Review and Reflect

Regularly assess your time management strategies. What's working, and what's not? Adjust your approach as needed.

Time Management Techniques

Several time management techniques can enhance your efficiency:

1. The Pomodoro Technique

This technique divides your work into intervals, traditionally 25 minutes in length, separated by short breaks. It helps maintain focus and prevent burnout.

2. The 2-Minute Rule

If a task takes less than 2 minutes to complete, do it immediately. It prevents small tasks from piling up.

3. Time Blocking

Allocate specific time blocks for related tasks. For example, set aside a block for answering emails and another for focused work. It minimizes distractions.

4. Eat the Frog

Tackle your most challenging or least enjoyable task first thing in the morning. This approach provides a sense of accomplishment and boosts motivation.

Time Management Tools

In the digital age, there are numerous tools and apps designed to aid in time management. Some popular ones include:

1. Google Calendar

A versatile digital calendar that allows you to schedule events, set reminders, and share calendars with others. It's accessible from various devices.

2. Todoist

A task management app that lets you create to-do lists, set deadlines, and prioritize tasks. It syncs across multiple platforms.

3. Trello

A project management tool that uses boards, lists, and cards to organize tasks and collaborate with others. It's excellent for team projects.

4. Focus@Will

A music service that provides background music designed to boost focus and

productivity. It's particularly useful for concentration during work or study sessions.

Challenges of Time Management

While effective time management is valuable, it comes with its challenges:

1. Distractions

Modern life is full of distractions, from social media notifications to the allure of streaming services. Staying focused is a constant struggle.

2. Lack of Discipline

Maintaining discipline in following your time management plan is not always easy. It requires self-control and commitment.

3. Unexpected Events

Life is unpredictable. Unexpected events can disrupt your carefully planned schedule.

4. Perfectionism

Striving for perfection in every task can lead to overcommitment and, paradoxically, inefficiency. Learning to accept "good enough" can be a challenge.

Conclusion

Effective time management is a skill that can transform your personal and professional life. By understanding the principles, techniques, and tools available, you can take control of your schedule and achieve more in less time. Remember that time is a finite resource, and how you manage it influences your success and well-being.

Chapter 8

YouTube Monetization Strategies: AdSense and Beyond

YouTube has not only revolutionized how we consume content but has also given creators a chance to turn their passions into a profitable endeavor. With the YouTube Partner Program (YPP), creators can monetize their channels and start earning money. The cornerstone of YouTube monetization is Google AdSense, but the strategies extend far beyond this partnership. In this chapter, we will explore the world of YouTube monetization and delve into the strategies that go beyond AdSense to help creators maximize their earnings.

Understanding the Basics

To kick start our journey into YouTube monetization, we must first understand the basics. AdSense is Google's advertising program that enables creators to earn money by displaying targeted ads on their YouTube videos. But how does it work?

1.1 AdSense and Revenue Sharing

Google AdSense operates on a revenue-sharing model. When you monetize your videos, Google places ads before, during, or after your content. You earn a portion of the ad revenue generated when viewers engage with these ads. The remaining part goes to Google.

1.2 Eligibility for AdSense

To monetize your YouTube channel through AdSense, you need to meet specific criteria, including having at least 1,000 subscribers and 4,000 hours of watch time in the past 12 months.

Beyond AdSense: Maximizing Monetization

While AdSense is the cornerstone of YouTube monetization, creators can enhance their earnings by diversifying their strategies. Let's explore some advanced approaches.

1.3 Channel Memberships

Channel Memberships allow your viewers to pay a monthly fee to become a member of your channel. In return, they get access to exclusive perks like custom emojis and badges. This not only provides a steady stream of income but also fosters a stronger sense of community.

1.4 Merchandise Shelf

YouTube offers the Merchandise Shelf feature, allowing you to showcase your merchandise directly below your videos. This is a great way to promote your brand and generate additional revenue.

1.5 Sponsored Content

As your channel grows, brands may approach you for sponsored content. This involves promoting or reviewing their products or services in your videos in exchange for payment. Sponsored content can be highly lucrative if you partner with relevant brands.

1.6 Crowdfunding

Platforms like Patreon and Kickstarter enable your viewers to support you directly. You can offer special rewards or content to patrons as a way of thanking them for their financial support.

1.7 Affiliate Marketing

By becoming an affiliate for various products or services, you can earn a commission for every sale generated through your unique affiliate links. This can be a great addition to your revenue stream.

Pitfalls to Avoid

As you explore monetization strategies beyond AdSense, it's essential to be aware of potential pitfalls.

1.8 Striking a Balance

While monetization is essential, bombarding your audience with ads or sponsored content can be counterproductive. Striking a balance between content and monetization is crucial.

1.9 Staying Compliant

Ensure that you adhere to YouTube's policies and guidelines when exploring different monetization options. Violating these can lead to demonetization or even the removal of your channel.

Conclusion

YouTube monetization is an exciting journey, and AdSense is just the beginning. By diversifying your strategies and engaging with your audience, you can transform your YouTube channel into a

profitable enterprise. Remember, it's not just about the money; it's about creating valuable content that resonates with your viewers.

In this chapter, we've scratched the surface of YouTube monetization strategies, but the world of possibilities is vast. Whether you're a budding creator or an established YouTuber, understanding

AdSense and exploring beyond it can help you achieve your monetization goals on YouTube. As you embark on this journey, remember that the key to success lies in producing engaging, high-quality content that keeps your audience coming back for more.

Chapter 9

YouTube Sponsorships, Affiliate Marketing, and Merchandise

YouTube monetization goes beyond traditional AdSense revenue. In this chapter, we'll explore the exciting worlds of sponsorships, affiliate marketing, and merchandise – three powerful strategies for YouTubers to boost their income while enhancing their relationships with viewers.

The Power of YouTube Sponsorships

Sponsorships are a pivotal aspect of monetization on YouTube. They involve partnering with brands and companies to promote their products or services within your videos. Here's why they're

essential:

2.1 Building Partnerships

Sponsorships allow YouTubers to build partnerships with brands that align with their content. These collaborations can lead to long-term relationships and ongoing income opportunities.

2.2 Diversifying Income

By incorporating sponsorships into your revenue strategy, you can diversify your income streams. Relying solely on AdSense income can be limiting, and sponsorships provide an excellent supplement.

2.3 Creating Value

Successful sponsorships are those that provide value to your audience. It's essential to choose products or services that resonate with your viewers, ensuring that your endorsements are credible and genuinely helpful.

Affiliate Marketing: Earning Commissions

Affiliate marketing is another potent tool in the YouTube monetization toolkit. It involves promoting products or services through unique affiliate links and earning a commission for every sale generated. Here's how it works:

2.4 Choosing the Right Partners

Selecting the right affiliate partners is crucial. It's best to promote products that you genuinely believe in and that your audience will find valuable.

2.5 Disclosing Affiliate Relationships

Transparency is essential in affiliate marketing. Be sure to disclose your affiliate relationships to your viewers, maintaining trust and credibility.

2.6 Diversifying Your Niche

Affiliate marketing enables you to diversify your content. By exploring a range of products and services, you can cater to a broader audience while maximizing revenue potential.

The Merchandise Shelf: Creating Your Brand

The Merchandise Shelf feature on YouTube allows YouTubers to showcase their branded merchandise directly below their videos. This is an excellent way to connect with your viewers and generate additional income.

2.7 Building Your Brand

Branding your merchandise is a fantastic way to engage with your audience. Your merch becomes a representation of your channel and can create a sense of belonging among your viewers.

2.8 Quality Matters

The quality of your merchandise matters. Investing in high-quality products ensures that your audience receives items they are proud to own, reinforcing their loyalty to your brand.

2.9 Promoting Your Merchandise

Promotion is key. Use your videos and other social media platforms to market your merchandise effectively.

Success Stories: YouTubers Who Mastered the Art

In this section, we'll delve into case studies of YouTubers who have excelled in sponsorships, affiliate marketing, and merchandise. We'll analyze their strategies and learn from their successes.

Avoiding Pitfalls

While these monetization strategies offer exciting opportunities, it's essential to be aware of potential pitfalls:

2.10 Authenticity Overload

Too many sponsorships, affiliate promotions, or merchandise pitches can make your content feel inauthentic. Striking a balance is essential.

2.11 Staying Compliant

Be sure to follow YouTube's policies and guidelines when using these monetization methods. Violations can lead to demonetization or the removal of your channel.

Conclusion

YouTube sponsorships, affiliate marketing, and merchandise are valuable tools for YouTubers to diversify their income and enhance their relationship with their audience. As you explore these monetization strategies, remember that authenticity and value are paramount. Building genuine relationships with your viewers is the key to long-term success in the world of YouTube content creation. So, go ahead, explore these strategies, and unlock the full potential of your YouTube channel.

Chapter 10

Building a Thriving YouTube Community: A Comprehensive Guide

In the ever-evolving realm of YouTube, establishing a flourishing community around your channel is more than just a dream—it's a tangible goal. But how do you go about it? This comprehensive guide will unravel the secrets to creating a dedicated following and growing your YouTube channel. We'll delve into audience demographics, interests, interaction through comments, live streaming, premiere events, collaboration, engaging with the YouTube community, user-generated content campaigns, viewer feedback, and measuring success. By consistently applying these engagement strategies and fostering a sense of belonging among your audience, you can chart a course towards YouTube success.

1. Understanding Your Audience

1.1 Audience Demographics

- Analyzing the Age, Gender, and Location of Your Viewers: The first step in building a thriving YouTube community is understanding who your audience is. Dive into the demographics of your viewers, discover their age, gender, and location, and tailor your content to match their unique characteristics.

1.2 Audience Interests
- Identifying the Topics and Video Types that Resonate with Your Viewers: Beyond demographics, it's essential to know what topics and video types your audience is passionate about. Create content that aligns with your audience's interests to keep them engaged.

2. Interaction Through Comments

2.1 Responding to Comments
- Why Responding to Comments is Essential: Your YouTube comments section is a direct channel for viewer engagement. Learn why responding to comments is crucial and how it can foster a sense of community.
- Tips for Managing and Engaging with Comments Effectively: Discover practical tips for handling comments, from addressing criticism gracefully to acknowledging positive feedback.

2.2 Asking Questions
- How to Encourage Viewer Participation through Questions: Engaging your audience through questions can spark conversations and keep viewers

coming back for more. Learn how to do this effectively.
- Using Polls to Gather Opinions and Preferences: Polls are a powerful tool for gathering viewer opinions and preferences, making them feel more involved in your channel.

3. Live Streaming and Premiere Events

3.1 The Power of Live Streaming
- Benefits of Live Streaming, such as Instant Feedback and Connection: Live streaming offers real-time interaction, instant feedback, and a unique connection with your audience. Explore the advantages and the steps to plan and promote live stream events effectively.

3.2 Utilizing Premiere Events
- Building Anticipation and Excitement through Premieres: Premiere events can create a buzz around your content. Learn how to use them to build anticipation and excitement.
- How to Engage with Viewers During Premiere Events: Make the most of premiere events by actively engaging with your audience during the broadcast.

4. Collaboration and Community Engagement

4.1 Collaborative Content

- The Advantages of Collaborating with Other Content Creators: Collaborations can introduce your content to new audiences. Discover the benefits and strategies for finding and approaching potential collaborators.

4.2 Engaging with the YouTube Community

- Participating in Community Forums, Groups, and Discussions: Engaging with the broader YouTube community can expand your reach and increase your exposure. Explore ways to actively participate in forums, groups, and discussions.
- Networking and Building Relationships with Fellow Creators: Building connections with other creators can lead to exciting opportunities and collaborations.

5. Promoting User-Generated Content

5.1 User-Generated Content Campaigns

- Initiating Challenges or Contests for Your Audience: Encourage your viewers to create and share content related to your channel. Learn how to kickstart user-generated content campaigns.

- Showcasing and Rewarding User-Generated Content: Showcase and reward the creative efforts of your audience to motivate them further.

6. Viewer Feedback and Channel Improvements

6.1 Collecting Viewer Feedback
- Methods for Gathering Feedback, such as Surveys and Polls: Listening to viewer feedback and making improvements based on their suggestions shows your commitment to your audience.
- How to Analyze and Prioritize Viewer Suggestions: Understand the best practices for collecting and prioritizing viewer feedback to enhance your content and channel.

7. Measuring Success

7.1 Evaluating Engagement Metrics
- Understanding Key Engagement Metrics and Their Significance: Tracking engagement metrics such as likes, comments, shares, and watch time is vital. Comprehend these metrics' significance and how they contribute to your channel's growth.

Chapter 11

Managing Your

YouTube Business

Running a successful YouTube channel goes beyond creating compelling content; it's also about effectively managing it as a business. In this chapter, we'll explore the key aspects of managing your YouTube business, from content planning to monetization strategies.

4. Content Planning and Strategy

4.1 Developing a Content Calendar

- The Importance of a Content Calendar for

  Consistency: A well-structured content calendar

  ensures a consistent posting schedule, keeping your

  audience engaged.

- Tools and Tips for Creating an Effective Content

  Schedule: Discover tools and tips to streamline the

content planning process and maintain consistency in your uploads.

4.2 Audience Analysis

- Understanding Your Audience's Preferences and Feedback: Getting to know your audience's preferences and feedback is crucial for tailoring your content to meet their expectations.

- Tailoring Content to Meet Your Audience's Expectations: Learn how to adapt your content to align with what your audience craves, ensuring their continued engagement.

4.3 Content Categories

- Categorizing Your Videos for Better Organization: Efficiently categorizing your videos aids organization and navigation for your viewers.
- How to Balance Various Content Categories to Keep Your Audience Engaged: Explore the art of balancing different content categories to maintain your audience's interest and variety in your content.

5. Video Production

4.4 Equipment and Editing

- Choosing the Right Equipment for Video Production: Selecting the appropriate equipment is essential for producing high-quality videos.

- Editing Techniques to Enhance Video Quality: Discover editing techniques to improve video quality and captivate your audience.

4.5 Collaborations and Outsourcing

- The Benefits of Collaborations with Other Creators: Collaborations can expand your reach and introduce your content to new audiences.

- When and How to Outsource Tasks like Editing or Graphic Design: Learn when and how to outsource tasks like video editing or graphic design to streamline your content creation process.

6. Channel Growth and Promotion

4.6 Audience Engagement

- Strategies for Engaging with Your Viewers Through Comments and Livestreams: Engaging with your viewers through comments and live streams fosters a sense of community and loyalty. The Power of Community Building: Building a strong community around your channel can lead to long-term success and support.

4.7 Promotion and Social Media

- Promoting Your Content on Social Media Platforms: Utilize social media to expand your content's reach and engage with a broader audience.

- Cross-Promotion with Other Creators for Mutual Benefit: Collaborate with fellow creators for cross-promotion, benefiting both parties and broadening your reach.

7. Monetization Strategies

4.8 AdSense and Beyond

- Understanding YouTube AdSense and How It Works: Delve into the workings of YouTube AdSense as a primary monetization option.

- Additional Monetization Options like Channel Memberships and Merchandise: Explore alternative monetization strategies, including channel memberships and merchandise, to maximize your revenue.

4.9 Affiliate Marketing

- Leveraging Affiliate Marketing to Generate Revenue: Learn how to incorporate affiliate marketing seamlessly into your content to generate additional revenue.

- Tips for Integrating Affiliate Links Seamlessly into Your Content: Discover best practices for integrating affiliate links without compromising the viewer's experience.

4.10 YouTube Sponsorships

- How to Attract Sponsorships from Companies: Attracting sponsorships is a lucrative way to monetize your channel. This section outlines strategies to secure sponsorships.

Best Practices for Delivering Sponsored Content to Maintain Trust with Your Audience: Learn how to maintain the trust of your audience while delivering sponsored content.

In this comprehensive guide, we've covered the crucial elements of managing your YouTube business, from content planning to monetization. By implementing these strategies, you can not only create captivating content but also cultivate a thriving and profitable YouTube channel.

Managing the Legal and Business Aspects of Your YouTube Channel

Managing your YouTube channel involves more than just creating content. You also need to navigate the legal and business aspects to ensure its success. In this guide, we'll explore essential topics in this domain to help you run your YouTube channel effectively.

4.11: Copyright and Fair Use

- Navigating Copyright Issues and Fair Use Policies: Understand copyright laws and fair use policies to ensure you don't infringe on others' content and protect your own.
- Protecting Your Content from Copyright Infringement: Learn how to safeguard your content from unauthorized use and copyright violations.

4.12: Financial Management

- Managing Revenue, Expenses, and Taxes as a YouTuber: Effectively handle the financial aspects of your YouTube business, including tracking revenue, managing expenses, and understanding tax implications.
- Budgeting and Financial Planning for Your YouTube Business: Develop a budget and financial plan to keep your YouTube business financially sustainable.

4.13: YouTube Analytics

- Understanding Key Metrics in YouTube Analytics: Explore essential metrics in YouTube Analytics to gain insights into your channel's performance.
- How to Use Data to Refine Your Content and Business Strategy: Leverage data from YouTube Analytics to make informed decisions and improve your content and business strategy.

4.14: Expanding Your Team

- Hiring and Managing a Team for Your YouTube Channel: When your channel grows, you may need a team. Learn how to hire, manage, and delegate tasks effectively.
- Scaling Your Business Operations Effectively: Ensure that your business operations can scale with your growing channel to maintain efficiency.

4.15: Diversification

- Strategies for Diversifying Your Online Presence and Income Sources: Explore methods to diversify your online presence and income streams beyond YouTube.
- Preparing for the Future of Your YouTube Business: Plan for the long term by preparing your YouTube business for changes and evolving trends.

Managing a YouTube channel as a business requires a combination of creativity, organization, and strategic thinking. By implementing the principles and practices outlined in this guide, you'll be well-equipped to manage your YouTube business effectively and take it to new heights.

Chapter 12

YouTube Monetization Policies and Guidelines: Demystifying YouTube Monetization

Introduction

YouTube offers content creators a vast opportunity to generate revenue through various monetization strategies. However, this potential comes with a set of policies and guidelines that creators must adhere to. In this guide, we'll explore the intricate world of YouTube's monetization policies, the guidelines you need to follow, and strategies for maximizing your earnings while staying compliant.

Section 12.1: Understanding YouTube Monetization

12.1.1: YouTube Partner Program (YPP)

What is the YouTube Partner Program?

The YouTube Partner Program (YPP) is your gateway to monetizing your channel. Itallows you to earn money from your videos through ads, channel memberships, and merchandise shelf.

Eligibility requirements and how to join To join the YPP, you need to meet specific eligibility criteria, including 1,000 subscribers and 4,000 watch hours in the last 12 months. Once eligible, you can apply for YPP through your YouTube Studio.

12 .1.2: Monetization Methods

Exploring different ways to monetize your YouTube channel Monetization methods on YouTube are diverse. You can earn through ads, channel memberships, and the merchandise shelf. Ads are the most common, with various ad formats like display ads, skippable video ads, and non-skippable video ads.

12.2: Monetization Policies

12 .2.1: Advertiser-Friendly Guidelines

What content is considered advertiser-friendly?

Advertiser-friendly content is safe, suitable for all audiences, and free from controversial or sensitive topics. Ensure your content complies with these guidelines by avoiding explicit language, violence, or controversial themes.

Tips for ensuring your content complies with these guidelines To maintain an advertiser-friendly status, review your content before uploading, and use YouTube's suitability checker tool to gauge if your video is likely to receive limited or no ads.

12 .2.2: Copyright and Fair Use

How to avoid copyright issues and fair use violations Prevent copyright issues by using only content you have the rights to, such as royalty-free music and your original creations. Understand fair use and give proper attribution when using copyrighted materials.

Dealing with Content ID claims

If you receive a Content ID claim, you can either remove the copyrighted content, replace the audio with YouTube's free audio library, or dispute the claim if you believe it's in error.

12 .2.3: Community Guidelines

The importance of adhering to YouTube's community guidelines Adhering to community guidelines is crucial to maintain a positive online environment.

Violations can result in warnings, strikes, or even channel termination.

Consequences of violating these rules

Violations can lead to penalties, including video removal, limited features, and strikes.

Three strikes can result in channel termination.

12 .2.4: Content Quality and Originality

The significance of high-quality, original content

High-quality, original content not only attracts more viewers but also advertisers. Focus on creating unique, engaging videos that resonate with your audience.

Avoiding duplication and low-value content Steer clear of duplicating others' content, creating spammy or repetitive content, or publishing low-value videos.

12 .3: Maximizing Monetization

12 .3.1: Audience Engagement and Watch Time

Strategies to boost audience engagement and watch time

Engage with your audience through comments, community posts, and live chats. Create compelling content that keeps viewers watching.

Their impact on monetization

Higher audience engagement and watch time contribute to increased ad revenue and algorithmic recommendations.

12 .3.2: Targeted Content and Audience

Tailoring content to attract a specific audience

Identify your target audience and create content that caters to their interests and needs.

The connection between targeted content and higher earnings

Relevant, targeted content can attract more loyal viewers and result in better monetization.

12 .3.3: Diversification of Income

Expanding your income sources beyond ads

Explore affiliate marketing, merchandise sales, and other monetization avenues to diversify your revenue streams.

12 .4: Staying Compliant

12 .4.1: Staying Updated

The ever-evolving nature of YouTube policies

YouTube's policies change over time. Stay informed by following YouTube's official

updates and guidelines.

Tools and resources to stay informed about changes

Use YouTube's Creator Academy and the YouTube Help Center to access valuable resources and stay updated on policy changes.

12 .4.2: Managing Strikes and Appeals

How to handle policy violations and strikes

If you receive a strike, assess the violation, rectify it, and learn from the experience to avoid future infringements.

The appeal process and best practices

If you believe a strike is unwarranted, you can appeal it. Provide a clear, concise explanation and evidence to support your case.

12 .5: Case Studies

12 .5.1: Successful Monetization Stories

Real-world examples of creators who have excelled in monetizing their content

Learn from successful creators like (mention specific creators), who have transformed their passion into a lucrative career through effective monetization strategies.

What you can learn from their experiences

Draw inspiration from their journeys and apply their strategies to your own content creation.

12 .6: Looking to the Future

12 .6.1: Future Trends in YouTube Monetization

Predicting the evolution of YouTube monetization

As YouTube evolves, be prepared to adapt to new monetization features and trends.

Keep an eye on emerging opportunities.

Preparing for new opportunities and challenges

Stay agile and open to embracing new opportunities while overcoming challenges that arise in the dynamic landscape of YouTube content creation.

In conclusion, YouTube monetization is a multi-faceted journey that requires a combination of quality content, compliance with policies, and effective engagement strategies. By understanding and implementing the guidelines provided in this guide, you can harness the full potential of YouTube as a revenue-generating platform for your content. Remember, YouTube monetization is not just about making money; it's about building a sustainable and successful online presence.

Conclusion

In this chapter, we've delved deep into the world of YouTube's monetization policies and guidelines. To succeed in monetizing your content, it's essential not only to create engaging and valuable videos but also to navigate the intricate policies that govern YouTube. By understanding these policies, following the guidelines, and continually adapting your strategies, you can harness the full potential of YouTube as a revenue-generating platform for your content. Remember, YouTube monetization is not just about making money; it's about building a sustainable and successful online presence.

Chapter 13

Tracking Your Progress and Analytics

In this chapter, we're going to dive deep into the fascinating world of tracking your progress and understanding YouTube analytics. Your journey on YouTube is a dynamic and evolving one, and having a keen eye on your channel's performance is paramount. Think of YouTube analytics as your compass guiding you through the vast terrain of online video content creation.

The Power of YouTube Analytics

Let's start with the basics. What are YouTube analytics, and why should you care?

What Are YouTube Analytics?

YouTube analytics are like your channel's report card. They provide data and insights about how your videos are performing. You can find a treasure trove of information on watch time, views, subscribers, and more. But it's not just numbers; it's the story of your channel's success.

Why Are They Essential?

YouTube analytics empower you to make informed decisions. Whether you want to refine your content strategy, understand your audience better, or maximize your revenue, analytics are your secret weapon. Ignoring them is like navigating through a dense forest without a map.

Understanding Key Metrics

Now that you're convinced about the importance of analytics, let's delve into some key metrics:

Watch Time

Watch time is the total number of minutes viewers have spent watching your content. It's a crucial metric for channel growth, as YouTube rewards channels with high watch time.

Views

Views are pretty straightforward; they count how many times your videos were watched. But they're more than just a vanity metric; they can give you insights into your video's popularity.

Audience Retention

Audience retention tells you how engaging your content is. It shows the percentage of your video that viewers typically watch. Higher retention is a good sign, indicating viewers enjoy your content.

Click-Through Rate (CTR)

CTR measures how many viewers click on your video when it appears in search results. A compelling thumbnail and title can boost your CTR.

Setting Goals and Objectives

Without a destination in mind, you're just wandering. It's essential to set goals and objectives for your YouTube channel. Whether you want to reach a specific subscriber count, increase watch time, or grow your revenue, having clear goals will guide your actions.

Fine-Tuning Your Content Strategy

Analytics are your best friend when it comes to refining your content strategy. By examining your most popular videos, identifying trends, and listening to your audience through comments and feedback, you can create content that resonates.

Audience Insights

Understanding your audience is a superpower. YouTube analytics provide data about your viewers, including their age, location, and interests. This information can help you tailor your content to your audience's preferences.

Monetization Insights

If you're in this for more than just fun (which is fantastic), you can also use analytics to track your earnings. Dive into your revenue reports and understand which videos are generating the most income.

The Power of Experimentation

Analytics allow you to experiment wisely. Try different video lengths, topics, and publishing times. Keep an eye on the analytics and adjust your strategy accordingly.

Staying Consistent

Consistency is the key to success on YouTube. Monitor your analytics regularly and use them to fine-tune your content and strategy. It's not about a one-time effort; it's about continuous improvement.

Celebrate Your Milestones

Lastly, don't forget to celebrate your achievements. When you reach a subscriber milestone, or your video goes viral, these moments are worth savoring. And guess what? Analytics can help you identify those turning points.

Conclusion

YouTube analytics are your guiding star on your YouTube journey. Embrace them, learn from them, and use them to elevate your content and grow your audience. As you dive into the world of

analytics, remember that it's a journey of continuous learning and improvement, and the insights you gain will empower you to become a better content creator.

So keep creating, keep analyzing, and keep reaching for the stars. Your YouTube adventure has only just begun.

Chapter 14

Troubleshooting Common Roadblocks

Welcome to Chapter 15, where we'll tackle the common roadblocks that every YouTuber faces on their journey. Creating content and growing your channel is a rewarding adventure, but it's not without its challenges. Let's dive into the most common roadblocks and how to troubleshoot them.

The Myth of Instant Success

One of the biggest roadblocks is expecting instant success. Many new YouTubers believe they can upload a video and wake up to millions of views. While it's possible, it's incredibly rare.

Building an audience takes time and patience. Don't be discouraged if you don't see rapid growth. Instead, focus on creating quality content.

Content Fatigue

Creating engaging content consistently can be exhausting. Content fatigue is a common roadblock, but it's also an opportunity to get creative. Try new formats, collaborate with others, and engage with your audience for fresh ideas. Remember, quality is more important than quantity.

The Dreaded Writer's Block

You sit down to script your next video, and… nothing. Writer's block is the enemy of all content creators. Combat it by stepping away, finding inspiration in other creators' work, or even seeking feedback from friends and followers. And don't be too hard on yourself; everyone experiences it.

Technical Glitches

From video editing software crashes to audio issues, technical glitches can bring your content creation process to a screeching halt. Troubleshooting these problems can be time-consuming, but investing in good equipment and learning the basics of video editing can help prevent many of these issues.

Stagnant Growth

Your channel's growth has plateaued. It's a frustrating roadblock, but there are ways to troubleshoot it. Analyze your analytics to understand what's working and what's not. Engage with your audience, collaborate with others, and consider updating older content to keep it relevant.

Burnout

Content creators often experience burnout, especially if they're juggling YouTube with other responsibilities. The key is balance. Set a content schedule that works for you, take breaks when needed, and don't feel pressured to churn out content if it's affecting your well-being.

Copyright and Legal Issues

Copyright claims and legal issues can be a major roadblock. Always use copyright-free music and images in your videos. If you receive a copyright claim, understand your rights and reach out to the claimant if necessary. Being informed can prevent these roadblocks.

Negative Comments and Trolls

Dealing with negative comments and trolls is part of the online world. The best way to troubleshoot this is to develop a thick skin. Focus on the positive feedback and remember that trolls thrive on attention. Don't feed them.

Financial Challenges

If your goal is to monetize your channel, financial roadblocks can be discouraging. Start small, invest wisely, and explore multiple income streams, like merchandise or affiliate marketing.

Remember, Rome wasn't built in a day.

Evolving Algorithms

YouTube's algorithms are ever-changing, and what worked yesterday might not work today. Troubleshoot this by staying updated on YouTube's guidelines and adapting your strategy accordingly.

Finding Support

Facing these roadblocks alone can be tough. Finding a supportive community of fellow YouTubers can be invaluable. Whether it's joining forums, Facebook groups, or attending YouTube meetups, connecting with like-minded creators can provide guidance and motivation.

Conclusion

Remember, roadblocks are part of the journey. Troubleshooting them is an opportunity for growth. So, don't be disheartened by the challenges you encounter. Embrace them, learn from them, and keep moving forward. Your journey as a content creator is unique, and overcoming these common roadblocks will make your story even more inspiring. Happy YouTubing!

Chapter 15

Celebrating Your Monetization Success

Congratulations! You've reached Chapter 15, and it's all about celebrating your monetization success. Making money on YouTube is a significant achievement, and it's time to bask in the glory of your hard work. In this chapter, we'll explore the different ways to revel in your monetization milestones and make the most of your earnings.

Reflect on Your Journey

Before we dive into the celebration, take a moment to reflect on your YouTube journey. Remember when you started with zero subscribers and views? Think about the challenges you overcame, the late nights editing videos, and the growth you've experienced. Celebrating your success is not just about the destination; it's about acknowledging the path you've walked.

Host a Milestone Livestream

Live streams are an excellent way to engage with your audience. Why not host a milestone live stream to celebrate reaching monetization? You can interact with your subscribers, answer their questions, and even do giveaways to show your appreciation. It's a great way to connect with your community.

Create a Thank You Video

Your viewers are the reason you've achieved monetization. Create a heartfelt "Thank You" video to express your gratitude. Share your journey, the challenges you faced, and how your audience supported you. Personal touches like this can strengthen your bond with your viewers.

Share Your Success on Social Media

Don't limit your celebration to YouTube. Share your monetization success on your other social media platforms. It's an opportunity to attract new subscribers and broaden your audience. Use eye-catching visuals and engaging captions to make the announcement stand out.

Plan a Giveaway

Celebrate your monetization by giving back to your audience. Plan a giveaway where you can offer prizes related to your niche. It's a win-win – you celebrate, and your subscribers get a chance to win something cool. Promote the giveaway across your social media platforms for maximum reach.

Attend Creator Meetups and Events

Monetization often grants you access to exclusive creator events. Take advantage of this opportunity to network with fellow YouTubers and industry professionals. It's a chance to learn, share experiences, and celebrate your success with others who understand the journey.

Upgrade Your Equipment

Investing in better equipment is a way to celebrate your monetization. Upgrading your camera, microphone, or editing software can improve the quality of your content. It's a tangible way to reinvest in your channel and demonstrate your commitment to your audience.

Set New Goals

Your monetization success is not the end but a milestone along the way. Set new goals for your channel. Whether it's reaching a certain number of subscribers, views, or revenue targets, having clear goals will keep you motivated and focused.

Engage Your Community

Engaging with your audience is key to continued growth. Interact with your subscribers through comments, live chats, and social media. A thriving community is something to celebrate every day.

Give Back to Charity

If you've reached significant monetization milestones, consider giving back to charity. Use your success to support a cause you're passionate about. Not only will you make a positive impact, but it's a wonderful way to celebrate your success with a purpose.

Conclusion

Monetization is a testament to your dedication and creativity. Celebrate this success in your unique way. Whether it's through a live stream, a heartfelt video, or investing in your channel's future, make the most of this milestone. Remember, your audience is your biggest cheerleader, so cherish the journey, because there are even greater successes ahead.

If you'd prefer we get your channel monetized within a month, or get you a Monetized Channel within a week, please send us a message to pokson68@gmail.com